Water Runs Through This Book

Water is beauty,
Water is life,

Nancy Bo Flood

Written by Nancy Bo Flood
Photographed by Jan Sonnenmair

FULCRUM PUBLISHING

Supported by Utah State University, NSF EPSCoR iUTAH, Cooperative Agreement NSF IIA-1208732, 5205 Old Main Hill, Logan, UT 84322. The views presented herein are those of the authors and do not necessarily reflect those of the National Science Foundation.

Additional photography: Shutterstock (outside back cover, robybret; p. 5, Dementevalulia; p. 6, Zffoto; p. 7, adike [top left], chromatos [top right]; p. 8, Andrea Danti [left], Anneka [right]; p. 10, Dragon Images; p. 11, decade3d - anatomy online [top], KPG Payless2 [bottom right]; p. 12, Meister Photos; p. 13, Naeblys [top]; p. 14, Designua; p. 15, MarcelClemens; pp. 16–17, Henri Vandelanotte; pp. 20–21, Mariday [center], witez77 [right]; pp. 24–25, lushik; pp. 26–27, Galyna Andrushko [spread], Kichigin [inset]; p. 28, Zern Liew [top], De Visu [lower left]; pp. 30–31, Volodymyr Doinyk; p. 32, S K Chavan; p. 33, Alan Mitchell [top], Everett Historical [lower right]; p. 36, Maria Jeffs; p. 37, Fulcrum Publishing [top]; CHEN WS [bottom]; p. 38, NorGal [bottom]; p. 39, Asaf Eliason; p. 40 Claudine Van Massenhove; p. 41, longtaildog [top]; p. 44, paul prescott [top], Gilles Paire [bottom]; p. 45, John Wollwerth; p. 47, smereka [bottom]; p. 48, Lewis Tse Pui Lung [top left], Pecoid [bottom]; p. 49, steve estvanik; p. 50, muratart; p. 51, De Visu [top], Tamara Kulikova [bottom]; p. 52, Tony Campbell; p. 53, Wollertz [top]; p. 54, Aron Brand; p. 55, Bruce C. Murray [top], Denis and Yulia Pogostins [bottom]; p. 56, DeepGreen [top], Joseph Sohm [bottom]; p. 57, Savvapanf Photo).

Library of Congress Cataloging-in-Publication Data

Flood, Bo.
 Water runs through this book / Nancy Bo Flood ; photographs Jan Sonnenmair.
   pages cm
  ISBN 978-1-936218-13-4 (paperback)
1. Water--Juvenile literature. I. Sonnenmair, Jan, photographer. II. Title.
 GB662.3.F627 2015
 333.91--dc23
                  2015009132

Printed in the United States of America
0 9 8 7 6 5 4 3 2 1

Fulcrum Publishing
4690 Table Mountain Dr., Ste. 100
Golden, CO 80403
800-992-2908 • 303-277-1623
www.fulcrumbooks.com

Many thanks to Bill and Barb Lorah for introducing the Flood Family to
both water and the desert. Forty years of friendship is still not enough.

—Nancy Bo Flood

To Eli and Eloise and all the children who will pass on the flow to the ones who follow.
Keep amazed, protect our resources, and keep splashing heartily in the water of life.

– Jan Sonnenmair

Contents

The Hoover Dam blocked the Colorado River and flooded the Mojave Desert, creating Lake Mead. Almost all the water for Las Vegas, Nevada, comes from Lake Mead.

Letter from the Author

IN THIS BOOK I SHARE THE WONDER OF WATER.

Water runs through our bodies, brings food and oxygen to our cells, and allows us to breathe, sweat, stand up, and move. Then water cleans up, taking away what pollutes and poisons.

Water is ever changing as it runs through, disappears, collects, and evaporates. Water freezes into glaciers, falls as a snowflake, drips from an icicle. Water stirs a spring seedling into life, drowns a delta, or quenches our thirst.

Water runs through our history, providing paths for human exploration. Rivers were our first highways, and along them we created cities and communities. Shores have been the beginning and ending place for travel, commerce, and war.

Water runs through countries, continents, and into oceans. Water creates watersheds—communities that connect us all. We are linked around the globe from beginning to end by water. Now, as we explore the universe for other planets, we search for the presence of water.

Water is life.

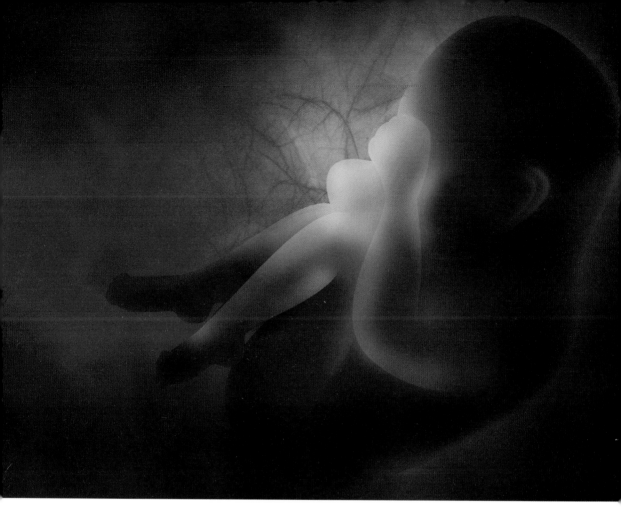

You Are Water

WATER WAS PART OF THE FIRST "breath" you took, inside your mother, long before you were born. While there, your lungs were actually filled with watery fluid, and blood full of oxygen and nutrients passed from your mother to you through your umbilical cord.

We begin in water, floating in an amniotic sea. We swallow before we learn to breathe—our first breath doesn't happen until the moment we are born. Our cells are bathed in water. As an embryo grows, blood vessels stretch out to form arteries, veins, and capillaries that carry watery-rich blood.

You are water—at least two-thirds of you. Even your bones! Water in the discs in your spine give support so you can stand, walk, and run.

Our body is a water machine. Only oxygen is as essential for life. Water keeps our bodies alive, fueled,

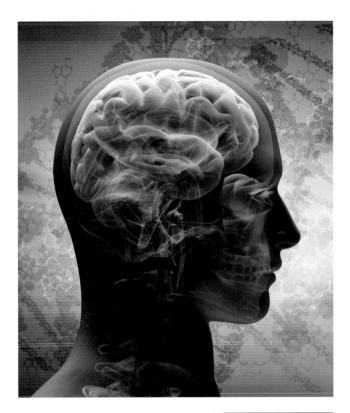

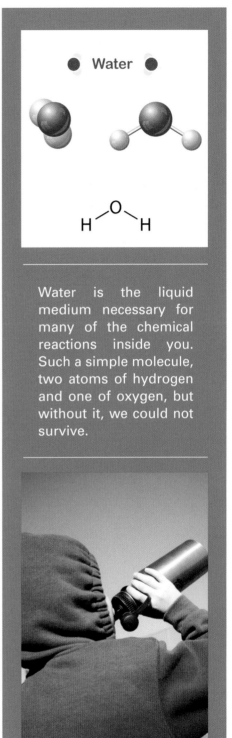

Water

H—O—H

Water is the liquid medium necessary for many of the chemical reactions inside you. Such a simple molecule, two atoms of hydrogen and one of oxygen, but without it, we could not survive.

and healthy. Feeling tired? Drink water. Lots of it. Every day we lose nearly twelve cups of water as we sweat, urinate, and breathe. Our lungs need to be moistened with water. Each day we exhale several cups of water. With water we grow new cells. Drink water—lots of it.

The water inside you is salty, like ocean water. And if this water dries up, what a lifeless raisin-kid, prune, mummy you would become!

The Pueblo people of the desert say, "Water speaks to water." We are water.

In this book we speak to water, and water speaks to us.

Your brain is mostly water. If you could count the molecules inside your head, eight out of ten would be water.

> "Tears are the medium of our most primal language in moments as unrelenting as death, as basic as hunger and as complex as a rite of passage."
>
> —Rose-Lynn Fisher,
> *Smithsonian Magazine*

The tears produced in lacrimal glands are made up of proteins, salt, and hormones. They are also almost exactly the same chemically as saliva.

In Weeping and Healing

WE CRY SEVERAL TYPES OF TEARS. Emotional tears remove chemicals that build up inside us when we are upset, sad, scared, or stressed.

Tears are not just water, they contain hormones and minerals that may be part of healing. One of those minerals is manganese. There is a theory that says too much manganese in our bodies affects our moods. While we always have manganese in our blood, when we are stressed, the amount of manganese increases. So, when we cry, our tears might have thirty times more manganese than normal. Perhaps crying helps take away the chemicals of sadness. Tears help heal the heart.

Tears have many functions. Tears also moisten our eyes. Lacrimal glands, little glands in the corners of our eyes, produce two types of tears: basal tears that lubricate our eyes and help prevent eye infections, and

Flamingos have very special tears—they are brimming with salt. These tall pink birds wade all day slurping up salty water to find their breakfast, lunch, and dinner. They filter-feed on algae and lots of tiny brine shrimp. Brine = salty water. Flamingos are one of the few land creatures that can drink salt water and live. That is because they excrete—get rid of—the deadly salt by "crying." As soon as salt levels get high enough in their bodies, flamingos expel it through salt glands above their eyes. Water and salty tears keep them alive and healthy.

When Water Weeps

Drops
Falling
From my eyes
Flow down my face
This is how
I say
I care

reflex tears that wash away irritants and dust. If our eyes are not kept clean, they won't work!

Water helps us cool down when we get too hot. Drinking a warm glass of water can energize, soothe a headache, and can relieve asthma. When you jump on a trampoline, do a cartwheel, or fidget at your desk, water is lubricating your joints. Water makes you flexible and full of energy.

If you don't drink enough water to replenish what you use, your body tries to hold on to, or retain water. Your hands and feet might swell. Your kidneys excrete less water so your urine becomes dark yellow. Dehydration—not enough water—makes you feel tired, achy, crabby, and even confused. You might not "know" you are thirsty. In a hot dry desert, even a few hours of hard hiking without water can be fatal. Someone needs to tell you: "Stop. Drink, now!"

Water also helps heal mind and soul. New studies show that our brain neurons are "hardwired" to respond to the sounds, smells, and feel of water. Relax in a hot bath, splash through a puddle, sit by a bubbling stream—your brain waves will show the calming effect of being near water.

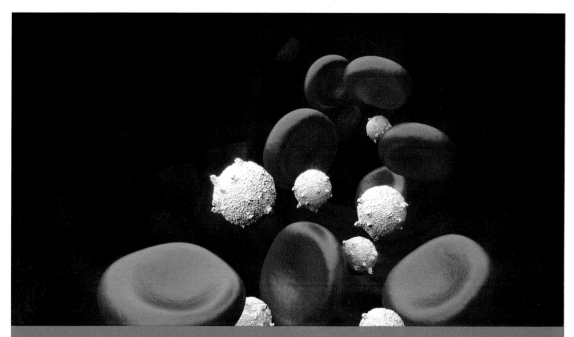

Water helps in other ways to heal us. Scrapes and cuts must be washed. Wounds must be cleansed. Water moves antibodies, nutrients, and hormones through the circulatory and lymphatic systems. As part of the immune system, water transports white cells to do battle at the site of an infection. Water is a unique liquid, a universal solvent or "mixer" that allows molecules to move, mingle, disconnect, reconnect, and reorganize. Water enables every part of your body to function efficiently.

Sen-No-Rikyu

When you hear the splash
Of water drops
Fall into the stone bowl
You will see
All the dust
Of your mind is
Washed away.

Washing your hands with soap and water is the most effective way to limit the spread of disease. Don't want to get sick? Wash your hands!

Find Water, Find Life

IMAGINE YOU ARE STANDING OUTSIDE. It is night. Look up. Search for an especially bright planet—perhaps Jupiter.

Can you see fish jumping on Europa, one of Jupiter's largest moons? Probably not, but the possibility that fish—or life—exists is not zero.

Despite what books and movies might have told us, our solar system is definitely not arid and empty. Our solar system is a watery place. In fact, astronomers are discovering that a "global ocean," perhaps one hundred miles deep, covers Europa. Is there life in that sea? Many comets have smashed into Europa, and comets carry organic, carbon-containing compounds.

Maybe there is life even farther away than our solar system. Look at those stars in the night sky. Each one is a sun. Some are like our own sun. Imagine planets circling those suns in distant galaxies. Astronomers are on the hunt to find evidence of water on those distant planets. Water might be found locked under a planet's surface like the water on Mars. If there is water, life as we know it is possible.

In the year 2000, the first conference on astrobiology—life on planets and stars—was held at NASA's research center. The first topic on the agenda? Water.

This illustration shows space probe *Voyager* flying near Europa, Jupiter's moon.

"Let there be work, bread, water, and salt for all."
—Nelson Mandela

Lost Lake, Oregon

Now imagine you are looking down, deep in the Earth—at least several hundred feet. Beneath the surface of our western deserts, hydrologists have found pockets of ancient water—water trapped during the last ice age. What's in it? No gum wrappers, no plastic water bottles, but instead particles that tell us what was happening on Earth more than ten thousand years ago! Who was drinking that water, swimming in it, pooping in it? Who knows, hydrologists might find a few front teeth from a saber-toothed cat or the fur from a woolly mammoth! Trapped ice-age water... a trip back in time.

Now look far north to the North Pole or far south to Antarctica. Glaciers and ice caps! Frozen water, frozen time. Looking at a glacier is being face-to-face with a piece of the earth's frozen history. Drill a core sample of this ice and discover clues about past ices ages, climate changes, or unknown aspects of our planet's history.

And as the glaciers—Antarctica's ice sheets—and polar ice caps melt, scientists are looking. Whose mitten will they find?

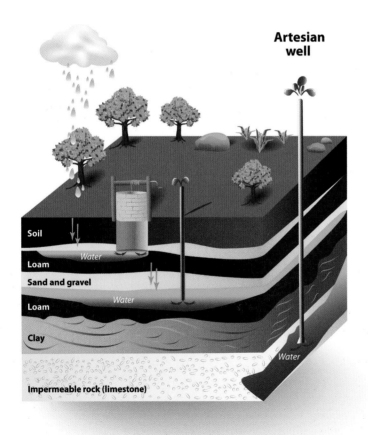

Artesian well

Soil

Water

Loam

Sand and gravel

Water

Loam

Clay

Water

Impermeable rock (limestone)

While groundwater can be replenished by waters trickling down from the surface, this happens very slowly. Many scientists believe that the water in large underground pools of water, or aquifers, dates back to the most recent ice age and probably earlier.

"Water is life's matter and matrix, mother and medium. There is no life without water."

—Albert Szent-Györgyi,
discoverer of Vitamin C

The Antarctic ice cap

Ice Skin, Winter Memory

Crackle of ice skin as I step, step, step
Snow melts, freezes, melts,
I spy a lost mitten
Left long-ago
By whom?

Glaciers cover about 10 percent of the Earth's surface. During the last ice age, they covered more than a third of the planet.

Water Powers Life

WHEN WATER DRIES UP and disappears, animals leave. People abandon their homes to thirsty ghosts. Deserts grow larger.

The definition of a desert is land that receives fewer than ten inches (25.4 centimeters) of rain over an entire year. Hold up a ruler. Now note the ten-inch mark—this would equal a desert's annual rainfall. During severe drought, rain might not fall for ten, fifty, or even five hundred years!

About one-third of our Earth is desert. But why am I talking about deserts in a book about water? In a desert the importance of water is crystal clear. A few inches of rain swiftly changes a desert's entire environment. Enough rain at the right time means healthy growth and enough food. Animals—domestic and wild—and people can survive.

But rain must come at the right time, in the right place, and in the right amount. If rainfall is too late or

too little, then plants wither and die. Too much rain can destroy roads, homes, and entire communities. Floods can wash away or drown the very life that needs water. In a desert we see clearly that water powers a cycle of plant growth that supports a healthy environment.

Let's look at the high desert of the Colorado Plateau. You are hiking down into the Grand Canyon, one of the largest canyons in the world. You have walked halfway down. You are thirsty. Your legs hurt. Your

During a desert drought, even the rocks get thirsty. Sandstone loses water during the hot, dry season of summer. When monsoon rains finally fall, water is reabsorbed into the rock, like a dry sponge soaking up moisture.

The Grand Canyon

Summer monsoon rains

feet burn. Your water bottle is empty. You are so thirsty you can't even swallow. Your throat feels stuck shut.

Meanwhile, only a few miles away thousands of gallons of water rush down the Colorado River. You can almost smell it, even hear it—cold, wet, thirst-quenching water.

In the high desert surrounding the Grand Canyon, there are different types of rain. The Navajo describe two kinds: male rain and female rain. Each has its own effect, sometimes supporting life, sometimes taking life.

Female rains produce gently falling showers. Moisture is slowly absorbed by thirsty sandstone or trickles into cracks, where it is "sipped" by the thirsty roots of pine, sage, and juniper.

Male rains fall during summer's monsoon season, harsh and furious. During the hot days of July and August, dark clouds pile high along the horizon. The air is still and feels ominous. Thunder booms, echoes,

The same rain also brings life. At sunset, after the deluge of a summer storm, canyon walls echo with a new song—toad song. Wherever puddles have appeared, spadefoot toads dig up through the mud where they have waited—maybe for months or even years—for rain.

Every male toad is calling, a seesaw baritone refrain, a symphony of rain song, of life song. Find a mate; lay eggs. Within a few weeks tiny tadpoles wiggle out and transform quickly into toads. Tails become legs with webbed feet that dig back down into the mud before the ground dries into hard earth.

and rumbles. Then the rains come. Sheets of water pour and pound. Roads turn into rivers. Red mud courses over boulders, slices paths between gulches, and then plunges like waterfalls over sandstone cliffs. Flash floods sweep away whatever is in their paths—boulders, trees, homes, and people. Male rain pours and rushes. Then stops.

Then, once again, streams disappear, waterfalls shrink to a thin trickle, and then... silence.

The desert waits for rain.

How long can you last without water? In the Grand Canyon or in any desert's dry, desiccating heat, you might last a day. Some hikers don't.

Water Is Not Always Wet

WATER IS AN EVER-CHANGING, MAGICAL CHAMELEON. Water can take many forms—as a solid, liquid, or gas (vapor). Whatever the form, water is still water: H_2O.

What is the color of water? Perhaps it's an intense liquid blue glowing with light. Blue like a bit of cold sky. Blue like turquoise. Scoop up a handful of clear blue water. Hold it and the blue is gone. It looks clear. Now imagine you are standing on a beach. Droplets of water in a stormy sky can paint a rainbow of colors. What is the color of water? The color of change.

What is the shape of water? The shape of a raindrop? A cloud? The shape of a puddle or an ice cube?

What is the size of water? As tiny as a dewdrop, a bubble on a gecko's chin, or as huge as an ocean? The Pacific Ocean is the biggest single "thing" on Earth. More than $2/3$ of the planet's surface is covered by water!

What words describe the smell of water? Putrid, stinking, polluted water? Or clean, clear, thirst-quenching water?

Listen to the sounds of water... rain coming, closer, faster, BAM! Rain pouring, drumming, gushing, rushing, and then the quiet drip and trickle as clouds move past, thin, disappear. Silence.

Water is not always wet. It rises invisibly as water vapor, a colorless gas. When water freezes, it has a very specific way of changing into a solid: it freezes first on the surface, allowing life "below" in rivers, lakes, and

ponds to continue. As water changes into a solid, it also expands into a variety of shapes, forming everything from snowflakes to ice cubes to icicles, or even immense ice caps. Ice sheets are frozen rivers of water. Glaciers are creeping mountains of water.

What a shape-shifting, amazing chameleon—water!

Look up. Feel the magic of a snowflake caught on the tip of your tongue. Listen to the thundering vibrations of water plunging down a waterfall. Imagine standing next to a glacier, a mountain of water. Maybe you will first need to make one...

The Perito Moreno Glacier in Santa Cruz, Argentina

Cerro Torre, Argentina

How to Make a Glacier

Capture
one
Snowflake.

Warm it, just a little.
The icy points evaporate,
Change

To water vapor
Invisible, but
Fills the space
Inside the snowflake.
Then the vapor cools,
Turns back to water,
Becomes the snowflake's frozen middle.

Now the snowflake is
A bit of glacier,
A tiny ball, no points, now called a firn,
A solid.

Find another million-zillion snowflakes.
Pile them high.
Take your time—
Fifty years or hundreds,
A million-zillion snowflake firns
Stacked up,
Press heavy
Squeeze out all the air
And become an

Ice-blue,
Ice-cold,
Glacier!

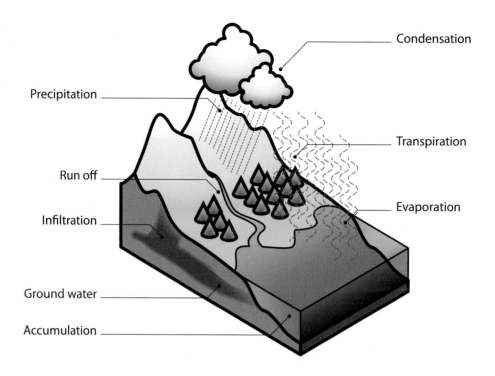

- Condensation
- Precipitation
- Transpiration
- Run off
- Evaporation
- Infiltration
- Ground water
- Accumulation

Water Movement, Cycles, and Impact

The biggest contributor to water pollution in the United States today is runoff water that carries pollutants from yards and fields.

ALL THE WATER THAT WAS ON THE EARTH back in the age of dinosaurs is still here for us.

It's the same water. Recycled.

We need to conserve this water and keep it clean. It's all we have.

The water cycle, perhaps the oldest form of recycling, involves both change and movement. Water recycling might begin with surface water—a puddle, pond, stream, or lake. The sun warms molecules on the surface of water. These molecules evaporate and become a gas—water vapor—and rise. Up high, the air is cooler, causing the vapor to condense into clouds. Air currents move the clouds, and when the water droplets in clouds become large enough, they fall as liquid rain, or as solid ice or snow.

After rain pours—or even mists or drizzles down—some rainwater is quickly recycled. However, fast recycling doesn't allow water to get clean. When rain pours over hard or impenetrable surfaces, such as

plowed fields, paved streets, and sidewalks, the water cannot be absorbed and instead gushes into storm sewers. This runoff water carries with it pollutants, pesticides, herbicides, fertilizers, and general grime from human use.

But water that falls on more porous, uncontaminated surfaces, such as forests, parks, or natural vegetated areas, soaks slowly into the earth. It often takes years before this water becomes part of surface water again. During the years it trickles down through layers of vegetation and earth, water is being "scrubbed clean."

This "biological Ferris wheel" of change, movement, and repeated interaction with an ecosystem is a natural cleansing process as well as a recycling system. How different rushing, uncleansed runoff water is from water that instead percolates. "Slow" water does not erode, gorge, or create gullies. The slow, natural cycling of water restores it to how we like it: water that is clean and clear.

"A single water molecule making its way through a stream-and-forest ecosystem is on a biological Ferris wheel. A raindrop may hit a leaf, trickle down the bark of a branch, evaporate to come down again as rain that flows into soil and is sucked up by a root hair and transpired from a leaf—to become part of yet another raindrop."
—Alice Outwater,
Water: A Natural History

Clearly, the water cycle is critically important for many reasons. First, the water is recycled. Second, the water is cleaned. Who would want to sit in a bathtub filled with dirty water? Or take a shower with 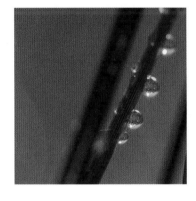 pesticides and herbicides pouring down? Third, water moves, often from places where it is not needed to places where it is badly needed. And fourth, water is stored, perhaps as part of the Earth's aquifers, in underground lakes, ponds, and rivers. Or it might be stored as snowpack, which acts like a type of "water bank." Winter's accumulation of snow will then melt slowly during spring to irrigate crops, forests, and wildflowers or to quench the thirst of many —people, livestock, and wildlife. Another storage system is ice. Icebergs and glaciers are mother lodes of fresh water!

Will we leave clean, clear water for the next era of dinosaurs?

A crucial aspect of the water cycle is the stabilization of our climate. Moisture that accumulates as glaciers, ice sheets, and ice caps not only provides a bank of freshwater but also a bank of cold air. Freezing, subzero temperatures create winds that help fuel air and ocean currents. These global currents keep moisture moving, which means water will again become rain—or snow—and will fall somewhere else, sometime later, where water is needed.

Imagine towing an iceberg to bring freshwater to areas of drought. There are people actually working to make iceberg towing happen!

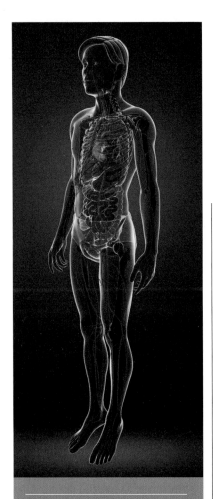

One Body, One Watershed

YOUR BODY IS A COLLECTION of diverse cells, each interacting with others to keep you alive, healthy, and well powered. Blood circulates throughout your body to near and distant cells, bringing nutrients and carrying away pollutants.

In New Mexico, people of the San Felipe Pueblo say:

**"The water in a watershed and
the blood flowing through the human body
are doing the same thing."**

Imagining our bodies as a biological watershed helps us understand the importance of each part of an environmental watershed. Water, not blood, is the main "connector."

Rain falls, washes into streams or soaks into the earth, and joins with water from many places to support an environmental community, a watershed. A watershed includes all the plants, animals—from dragonflies to grizzly bears—and people that depend on the moisture that falls or flows in one area. The moisture below- and aboveground forms a community, all parts linked by the need for and use of water. Each watershed is unique: an interaction and interdependence of earth, plants, and animals, including people.

Think like a watershed. You are more than 70 percent water. Your health is dependent on the health of your watershed.

Water lives in water.

Your body is like a watershed—a system of interconnecting and interdependent parts, each contributing to the health of the whole, each impacted by the functioning of other parts. If your brain stops thinking, the rest of your body is in big trouble. If your heart stops pumping, disaster is imminent.

"Canyons are basically nets that catch water. Branches and fingers and tributaries scour the land above, sending everything down, so that when a storm passes, all of its rainwater is driven toward a single point. Water can run from tens of miles down hundreds of feeder canyons, spilling into deeper and deeper, fewer and fewer canyons until the volume of the flood has jumped exponentially into one final chasm where everything converges."

—Craig Childs,
The Secret Knowledge of Water

Dead Horse Point, Utah

"As man has within him a pool of blood wherein the lungs as he breathes expand and contract, so the body of the earth [h]as its ocean, which also rises and falls every six hours with the breathing of the worlds."
– The Notebooks
of Leonardo da Vinci

In Laughter and Play

In every part of the world
Water is play.

Dive right in, splash, float,
Or bring along a pole and fish.

Dash through a sprinkler,
Walk in the rain.

Sit by a meandering river.
Wash your horse!

Water makes us laugh.
And when you're tuckered out,

Take a bath.

Maxwell Canyon, Utah

"Cleanliness is half of faith."
– Muhammad to followers

Water Is Sacred, Water Is Ceremony

WILMA MANKILLER WAS AN ACTIVIST and the first female chief of the Cherokee Nation. For Wilma, "going to water" meant home, family, and a healing place of prayer. In the high desert mesas of the Southwest where Pueblo people have lived for centuries, here also, water means home—one's place in the world.

For the Pueblo people of the Southwest, water is scarce and precious. Their prayers often revolve around water. In times of scarcity they communicate with water: "It was time to ask the cloud people for help. It was time to ask for their love—to ask for rain."

Throughout human history and in all parts of the world, water is part of rituals of change, cleansing, and healing.

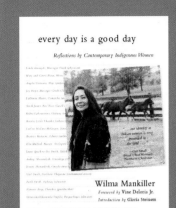

"The Mankiller family land defined who I am... The land held deep memories of my family... my siblings and I gathered water from a cold spring where my grandparents had also stored melons, fresh milk, and butter. We shared that spring with bobcats, mountain lions, wild pigs, and an occasional deer. ... It is my favorite place to pray.

The spring was probably used by my grandparents for Cherokee medicine that required 'going to the water'... it was said that dipping into water seven times during the fall when leaves fell into the water promoted healing."

—Wilma Mankiller
Every Day Is a Good Day

"When you tie the girl's hair, tie it straight, like rain."
– Watershed

The Yao people live in southern China. Traditionally, Yao women wash their hair only in the summer and autumn. Before 1987, in the Yao culture, the only time that a man would be allowed to see a woman's hair long and uncovered was if he were married to her, and then, only on their wedding day.

A water ceremony in Lake Atitlan, Guatemala

Navajo and Apache people wash the hair of a young girl and "reshape" it to symbolize her change from child to womanhood.

In many cultures and places around the world, water is a symbol of cleansing and key transitions—spiritual, physical, or emotional—from birth until death.

Christians baptize with water. Babies or adults are dunked in holy water so that any stain of sin is washed away. Sacred cleansing brings body and soul into new life.

In Japan, as part of the ancient Shinto ritual called Misogi Shuho, a person "washes" under the sacred waterfall at the Tsubaki Grand Shrine. To stand fully and unprotected under the thundering power of falling water celebrates the oneness of worshipper, water, and the creative life force of the universe.

Water runs through our lives from birth to death.

Shinto believers rinse their mouths and clean their hands at purification fountains.

"We honor water every day. It's in our prayers, it's in our songs. It's in our symbols. … The lightning bolt, the rain, the rainbow represent water. Even our hair. When we have ceremonies, women leave their hair long and straight because that represents water."

– Rina Swentzell,
Watershed

"When there is a river in your growing up, you probably always hear it."
– Ann Zwinger

The washing of the dead is a sacred part of letting go, acknowledging a person's passage from this life to another. In India at the holy river of Ganges, Hindu people who are very ill or dying bathe in the river. The ashes of the dead are scattered over this holy river.

– National Geographic

Most people in the United States use about one hundred gallons of water each day. People who do not have running water use fewer than five gallons a day. Every gallon must be carried. One gallon of water weighs 8.3 pounds (3.76 kg). Hold that on top of your head and walk around for a few hours. Not fun! How much water would you use if you had to carry every drop? For one whole day keep track of each time you turn on a faucet. Figure out how much water you use.

Walking for Water

OF THE 7 BILLION PEOPLE in our world, about 1 billion spend most of their day collecting and carrying water, a combined sum of more than 200 million hours each day.

Women and children. No time to play. No time for school. The only way to get water is to walk. Something to think about next time you walk to the kitchen and turn on a faucet.

What is the source of the water you use each day? The water that flows through underground pipes into your home—where does that water come from? Water—we use it all the time but seldom think about it. It's almost invisible to us. But think about this: What if you turn on the faucet and nothing comes out? Flush the toilet. No water there either. Hmm. Try all the faucets in the house and school. Nothing! Where will you go to get a drink? Or wash your hands? Where does your water come from?

If you can't get water by turning on a faucet, where would you get it? What about this? People who live in the driest desert on Earth use huge nets to catch fog and "harvest" water. The Atacama in Chile is an absolute desert—the most barren and stark of all desert environments—but more than 1 million people

Moon Valley, the Atacama Desert

Add up all the miles women and children in South Africa walk
    For water.
        Every day.
Sixteen trips to the moon and back,
        Every day,
            For water.

Many children, often from the time they are only five years old, spend their whole day walking for water. Walking for water for drinking, cooking, washing, and for watering cattle, camels, or goats. Walking for water to stay alive.

A Navajo woman herds her family's sheep to find water and grazing lands.

live there, grow food, and survive by capturing the moisture in fog.

A Navajo family with running water uses about sixty gallons a day, but families who haul water use only twelve.

Oh, for a faucet, just turn the handle and have all the water you want. Or to have a backyard or a village pump, push the handle up and down, and clean water flows out! Then children could play; children could go to school. Clean water also means not feeling sick half the time from drinking contaminated water.

Water is one of our most valuable resources. How often we just let it run down the drain.

Next time you flush the toilet or turn on a faucet, think about where that water came from. As it disappears down a pipe, where does it go? We are "rich" in running water and seldom think about how much we use... how much we waste.

In some desert areas, such as the southwestern United States, people haul water from a central community well. Ranchers on the Navajo Nation use windmills to pump up water from aquifers deep underground. They fill huge plastic containers and haul it to their grazing livestock—sheep, goats, cattle, and horses—and for home use—cooking, cleaning, and drinking.

Boys in Dehli, India, fill containers with drinking water to carry back home.

Humanitarian workers install a pump in a remote area of Burkina Faso.

Besides the hundreds of gallons used in homes every day, millions of gallons are used to produce our food, shoes, clothes, electricity—even our computers. Strange to think how wealthy we are because we have water.

What can we do to make water available to everyone?

One thing is to learn about organizations that are drilling wells for communities that are without water.

Read *A Long Walk to Water* by Linda Sue Park. It's a terrific book, and a short one. In the back is a description of Water for South Sudan, Inc. (www.waterforsouthsudan.org). This nonprofit organization has been drilling dozens of water wells in South Sudan for communities without water. The founder, Salva, is a survivor of the Lost Boys who walked from Ethiopia to Kenya to survive the Second Sudanese Civil War (1983–2005). With the help of several international organizations such as the United Nations and the International Red Cross, Salva was finally able to leave his "home," a refugee camp, and live with a family in the United States. *A Long Walk to Water* is Salva's story.

Maybe if your school, church, or scout group read *A Long Walk to Water*, they would want to work together to raise money to drill a well in South Sudan.

Imagine making a change in the world so that the children of one entire village would no longer need to walk to the moon for water.

Women in Sudan pump water from a well that was installed in their community.

Efficient irrigation systems decrease water consumption.

Making Supper and Shoes

THE TWO LARGEST CONSUMERS of water are agriculture—growing food—and mining and manufacturing—digging resources and then making things.

In other words, water is used to grow your supper and make your shoes.

Whatever you eat comes from something grown—grass, corn, cows, chickens, pigs, fish, octopi, and even chocolate! Water is needed to grow and produce food. About 70 percent of the world's water is used for growing food. Thus, no water, no supper. Thirsty chickens stop laying eggs. Cows stop making milk. Corn doesn't tassel. Hay withers.

In the western United States, agriculture consumes more water than any other activity. But conservation practices do work. Crops that require less water obviously use less water. What else makes a difference? What we choose to eat does. In the United States we like to eat foods that require a high use of water.

A healthy way to conserve water is to eat more plants: grains, vegetables, and fruit. Less water is needed to grow corn, wheat, or rice than to raise cattle or pigs.

The other major consumer of water is mining and manufacturing.

A lot of water is necessary to manufacture "things," such as the shirt you are wearing. That shirt? About 700 gallons. Those new shoes? At least 2,000 gallons. The more stuff we buy, the more water is used to make more stuff.

Water is an essential part of almost every industry. Every type of mining requires large amounts of water. Thousands of gallons of it are needed to produce gas, coal, and oil so you can ride to school in comfort or stay warm during winter. Following the passage of the Clean Water Act in 1972 (the Federal Water Pollution Control Act), both the mining and manufacturing industries changed their methods in order to use far less water—a reduction of up to 50 percent! Conservation strategies really do make a difference.

How much water does it take to make a hamburger? Take a guess—10...50...maybe 100 gallons of water? Try 4,000–18,000 gallons for one thick, juicy hamburger. It takes a lot of water to "grow a cow," transport the cow to the butcher, process the meat, ship the hamburger to a store, cook it, and then clean up the kitchen.
How much water would you be willing to carry to eat one hamburger?

Ripe corn prior to harvest. To eat an egg or one pound of corn takes more than 100 gallons of water. A slice of bread takes only ten gallons.

Conservation can start right at home. Use less energy, then less water is needed to make more energy. In the winter, turn down the thermostat a few degrees. In the summer, open windows, or turn on a fan rather than an air conditioner. Walk or bike rather than drive. Or, take the bus, light rail, or subway. Better yet, ride a horse!

Don't leave water running when you're fixing a meal, brushing your teeth, or washing your face. Turn off the shower while washing your hair. Take fewer baths. Maybe only once a month? Just kidding. But imagine not taking a bath for a month because there is no water to spare.

Many kids in the world have no choice. Having water means walking for water. That precious water is used for drinking, cooking, and for keeping livestock—sheep, goats, cows, or camels—alive.

For more actions you can do to conserve water, head to the end of this book.

At this small gold mine in Chicken Creek, Alaska, workers wash gold out of rock and sand.

Young girls learning to carry water in Orissa, India

Having sufficient irrigation rights—enough water when water is needed—means having hay to sell, dairy cattle to milk, or sheep to shear. Water means profit and survival.

Going, Going... STOP!

WATER BELONGS TO EVERYONE.

Or does it?

Not in the southwest United States. Water is sold, stolen, legislated, and fought over. Ranchers have waged wars over water. Water courts are filled with legal fights over water.

One of the biggest challenges to our country's economy and environmental health is water conservation—individuals and communities as well as farms, ranches, businesses, and manufacturers all using less water.

Underground water, Earth's aquifers, is the largest source (more than 90 percent) of clean, usable water. Just ask a dinosaur. Depleting these invisible reserves —our "savings account" of water—is asking for trouble,

Who has first rights to this limited resource? Water laws that govern rights and usage are changing. One reason is the critical need to decrease consumption. Another is the need to protect both surface water and groundwater from pollution and depletion.

A mountain reservoir following several years of drought.

Gran Canaria,
Barranco de Aldea

During a drought, the entire watershed community changes. Think about all the animals that come to water to drink and eat, rest and dream.

big time. Aquifers takes years, even centuries, to fill. Once emptied, they are gone. If polluted with heavy metals or nondegradable wastes, they can become poison. Deep wells and overuse threaten to deplete this essential water supply.

Another part of water conservation is preserving or restoring free-flowing rivers. When a river or lake dries up, not only does the body of water itself die but all the layers of life in that watershed die or leave—fish and insects, trees, birds, grasses.

All levels of conservation acts, from legal ones at the federal and state levels to individual actions, are making a difference. Several states, including Minnesota and Colorado, have passed legislation to protect rivers. Streams have "first rights" so water continues flowing. No longer can agriculture or industry use water until a river runs dry. In recent years, average home water use in this country has decreased from two hundred to one hundred gallons of water per person daily. Individuals are figuring out effective ways to clean up the ocean!

Sometimes the job of conservation seems overwhelming, impossible to make a difference. Can one person make a difference? Of course. You can. Each one of us can make a difference every day. We are all in this world's watershed together.

Pine beetles prey on drought-stricken trees such as in this forest in South Dakota, killing millions of trees each year.

What can you do? Take action, one drop, one bucket, one project at a time.

A dust storm in Colorado

At Home

Across the nation, more than 1 trillion gallons of water a year are wasted just through household leaks. This is as much water as 11 million households would use in a year.

1. Turn off the faucet when brushing your teeth. Save 25 gallons a month.

2. Turn off the faucet when washing your hair. Save 150 gallons a month.

3. Shorten shower time by two minutes. Save another 150 gallons.

4. Find any leaky faucets or toilets, so your family can get them fixed. A leak can waste more than 10,000 gallons of water a year.

5. Run the clothes washer and dishwasher only when full. How much water does that save in just one month? One thousand gallons!

6. Keep a bucket in the kitchen and bathroom. Use "gray water"—water from washing dishes or taking a bath —and water plants.

7. Even consider "mellow yellow": Talk to your parents about having a no-flush/later-flush toilet policy. Mellow yellow... wait to flush.

8. Learn about xeriscaping—planting only drought-resistant, low-water-use plants. Maybe your parents will join in, maybe neighbors or your classroom— your entire school! Reduce outside water use by 60 percent.

If a xeriscaped yard is well planned, it doesn't just use less water than regular landscape. It will also require less maintenance such as weeding, fertilizing, pest control, and pruning.

At School

Help bring water to people who walk for water every day. Imagine your class or school working together to raise money to drill a well for such a community. Then kids there would not have to walk for water—they could go to school.

Interested? Suggest to your class that everyone read *A Long Walk to Water,* described in the "Walking for Water" chapter.

> "Water is something we all have in common.
> It bridges our different walks of life. And its fragility is our fragility."
> – Alexandra Cousteau, environmental advocate
> and granddaughter of Jacques Cousteau

In Your Community or School

One day a week—or month—have everyone walk, bike, take a bus, or carpool to school.

Design and plant a school garden. Create green "water recycle" areas.

Is your school composting? Recycling plastics and glass? Find out.

Keep learning about water. Keep talking about water. Express yourself as you share your ideas: Create poems, posters, songs, and reports about water. Increase water awareness in your own home and classroom. Awareness creates caring, and caring creates conservation ideas. Every single drop decreases water use.

Water is the lifeblood of both the people and the environment. If we bleed our wells, rivers, and aquifers dry, where will we get more water?

Organizing a bike day doesn't just conserve energy. It can also be a great opportunity to host a fund-raiser.

Water Is Beauty

THE NAVAJO PEOPLE SHARE THIS STORY: Earth fell in love with Sky, and Sky with Earth. There was such joy! Their happiness filled the clouds with laughing, splashing rain.

What is it about water that makes people everywhere pause to listen and watch? In parks we look for ponds or a meandering creek. In cities we build fountains. Children laugh as they splash in the cool spray. Couples stroll and stand hand in hand, watching water. Elders listen to the sounds of flowing water and remember. Water invites us to stop and reflect, and when we do, we feel refreshed. Often we experience a sense of wonder. In the evening on a beach, people watch the colors of the sea change from ruby-red to indigo. We wait in silence as a full moon rises through the silver mist shrouding a volcanic lake.

And in the end, perhaps beauty is water's deepest mystery.

And so, thank you, for listening, reading, and thinking about water...

Water talking with water.

References

General Books and Articles

Ball, Phillip. *Life's Matrix: A Biography of Water.* Berkeley: University of California Press, 2001.

Carlson, S. *Bringing It Home: Elements of Effective Diverse Education. Honoring the Past, Embracing the Present, Teaching for the Future.* Bluff and Salt Lake City: Four Corners School of Outdoor Education, iUTAH, 2012.

Childs, C. *The Secret Knowledge of Water.* New York: Little, Brown and Company, 2000.

Childs, C. *Apocalyptic Planet.* New York: Pantheon, 2012.

Folger, Tim. "Rising Seas." *National Geographic,* September 2013, pp. 30–57.

Grace, Stephen. *Dam Nation, How Water Shaped the West and Will Determine Its Future.* Guilford, CT: Globe Pequot Press, 2012.

Gray, S. "Earth's Water Is Too Precious a Resource to Waste." *The Sopris Sun,* June 20, 2013, p. 9.

Green, E. "Tunneling Under California's Water Wars." *High Country News,* August 20, 2013, pp. 3, 5.

Keller, S. J. "Dry News From the Water Mines." *High Country News,* July 22, 2013, pp. 6–7.

Kingsolver, B. "Fresh Water." *National Geographic,* April 2010, pp. 36–49.

Koch, W. "High and Dry in Texas." *USA Today,* July 10, 2013, pp. 1, 5.

Loeffler, J. *Thinking Like a Watershed.* Albuquerque: University of New Mexico Press, 2012.

Mankiller, Wilma. *Every Day Is a Good Day.* Golden, CO: Fulcrum Publishing, 2004.

Miller, J. "Water Rights." *High Country News,* June 24, 2013, pp. 12–17.

Outwater, Alice. *Water: A Natural History.* New York: Basic Books-HarperCollins, 1996.

Salina, Irena, ed. *Written in Water.* Washington, DC: *National Geographic,* 2010.

Zaffos, J. "The Great Runoff Runaround." *High Country News,* July 23, 2013, pp. 7–9.

Children's Books and Articles

Bremmer, Larry Dane. *Glaciers.* New York: Children's Press, 2000.

Gowan, Barbara. *D Is for Desert.* Ann Arbor, MI: Sleeping Bear Press, 2012.

Gray, Rita, compiler, and Rayan O'Rourke, illustrator. *One Big Rain, Poems for Every Season.* Watertown, MA: Charlesbridge, 2010.

Hoffman, Mary. *Earth, Fire, Water, Air.* New York: Dutton Children's Books, 1995.

Hutchinson, Caroline. *The Water Cycle.* Pelham, NY: Network Learning, 2011.

Kerley, Barbara. *A Cool Drink of Water.* New York: Scholastic, 2002.

Kraul, Walter. *Earth, Water, Fire, and Air.* Edinburgh: Floris Books, 1984.

Lyon, George Ella, Katherine Tillotson. *All the Water in the World.* New York: Atheneum, 2011.

Mora, Pat. *Water Rolls, Water Rises: El Agua Rueda, El Agua Sube.* CBP Books, 2014.

Park, Linda Sue. *A Long Walk to Water.* New York: Houghton Mifflin, 2010.

Rockwell, Anne. *Clouds.* New York: HarperCollins, 2008.

Salas, Laura Purdie. *Water Can Be...* Minneapolis: Millbrook Press, Lerner Publishing, 2014.

UNICEF. *A Life Like Mine, How Children Live Around the World*. New York: DK Publishing, 2002.

Walker, Sally. *Glaciers*. Minneapolis: Lerner, 2008.

White, Dianne. *Blue on Blue*. Simon and Schuster, 2014.

Woodward, John. *Eyewitness Water*. New York: DK Publishing, 2009.

Videos

Center for Global Environmental Education, Hamline University. *Water Down the Drain*. St. Paul, MN, 2013.

Center for Global Environmental Education, Hamline University. *Life and Death on the Mississippi*. St. Paul, MN, 2010.

Center for Global Environmental Education, Hamline University. *The Urban Water Cycle*. St. Paul, MN, 2009.

Center for Global Environmental Education, Hamline University. *Waters to the Sea: The Chattahoochee River*. St. Paul, MN, 2004.

Center for Global Environmental Education, Hamline University. *Waters to the Sea: Trinity River*. St. Paul, MN, 2010.

The Cherokee Word for Water. Based on a true story about Wilma Mankiller, first modern woman to serve as Chief of the Cherokee Nation, 2013.

McKibben, Bill, and Sylvia Earle. *Written in Water: Messages of Hope for Earth's Most Precious Resource*.

Redford, Robert. *Watershed: Exploring a New Water Ethic for the New West*. Sundance: Kontent Films, 2009.

Santa Fe Productions and Tim Aydelott Productions. *Valles Calders: The Science*. Santa Fe, NM, 2013.

Websites

www.nationalgeographic.com/freshwater/
Freshwater crisis

www.circleofblue.org/waternews/
Water news

www.ecobusinesslinks.com/rainwater-harvesting.htm
Rainwater harvesting

www.greatgarbagepatch.org/
Plastics and pollutants

www.waterforpeople.org
Improving drinking water

www.centerforwateradvocacy.org
Promoting water availability

http://www.psi.org/health-area/water-sanitation/#about
Waterborne diseases

http://www.globalwaterchallenge.org/
Accessing clean water

http://water.usgs.gov/edu/watercycle.html
Water cycle

www.waterforsouthsudan.org

water.usgs.gov/edu/watercycle.html

www.facebook.com/Somebodycares.malawi

Glossary

amniotic – describes the fluid or sac in which an embryo or fetus of a reptile, bird, or mammal develops prior to being born or hatching

antibody – a substance a body produces to fight disease

artesian well – an underground well from which pressurized water rises to the surface of the Earth

carbon – a common element, found in all living plants and animals, which combines with other elements such as nitrogen and oxygen; in its pure state, carbon is found in diamonds and graphite

circulatory system – a system of organs and tissues that moves blood throughout a body; includes the heart, blood, blood vessles, and lymph vessels and glands

composting – fertilizing soil using a mixture of decaying organic substances such as dead leaves or manure

condense – to change from a gas or vapor to a liquid or a solid form, such as when steam becomes water droplets

conservation – the action of protecting and preserving natural places; the action of using a natural resource in such a way that it is not depleted

core sample – a cylindrical section that is drilled out of a substance that occurs naturally, such as of layers of rock or ice

desiccating – thoroughly drying, dehydrating

ecosystem – a system or network of living organisms and elements that occur in an environment

environment – the air, water, minerals, organisms, and other factors (such as weather) that surround and affect any organism at any time

filter-feed – to feed or gain nutrition from particles that are strained out of water by circulating the water through an animal's body

flash floods – a sudden, often destructive, rush of water that moves quickly through a canyon or riverbed following a heavy rainfall

hormones – a substance that a body produces and that travels through the bloodstream to certain organs or tissues in order to effect their activity or function

hydrologists – scientists that study the circulation, distribution, and properties of water on Earth and in the atmosphere

ice age – cold periods during which glaciers covered much of the Earth; the most recent ice age ended about 10,000 years ago

iceberg – a large mass of ice that has detached from a glacier and is now floating in an ocean or sea

ice cap – a thick layer of ice covering a large area of land

immune system – a complex system of the body, made up of cells and tissues, that protects a body from infection and foreign substances, and that destroys infected or sick cells in a body

irrigate – to divert streams, flood, or spray dry land to supply it with water

lymphatic system – a system of the body that makes, holds, or carries a colorless fluid that is mostly made of white blood cells

manganese – a hard, grayish white metal that is chiefly used as an alloy that makes steel strong

mesas – a hill or mountain that has steep sides and a flat top

molecules – the smallest physical unit that is made up of identical atoms; molecules combine to make element or compounds

monsoon – a seasonal weather pattern that commonly brings heavy rains

neurons – a specialized cell in the nervous system that carries nerve impulses

nondegradable – describes a substance that cannot decompose or degrade

organic – describes a substances that comes from an animal or vegetable origin; something that occurs naturally

sandstone – a commonly found sedimentary rock that is mostly made of sand and quartz

solvent – a substance that can dissolve another substance

symbol – something such as a letter, word, or picture that represents something else

Index

About the Author and Photographer

Nancy Bo Flood is an author, psychologist, teacher, and mother who writes about what she enjoys—children and foreign cultures. She has taught around the world, including Japan, Saipan of Micronesia, Hawaii, and Samoa. Nancy received her Ph.D. from the University of Minnesota and continued her research at London University as a post-doctoral fellow. More recently she earned a MFA from Vermont College of Fine Arts. She currently lives on the Navajo Nation in northern Arizona.

Jan Sonnenmair is an award-winning, Portland, Oregon-based commercial and documentary photographer who focuses her work on women, children, and social issues around the world. Sonnenmair helps NGOs, corporations, universities, and publications tell stories with imagery.